COUNTRY EXPLORERS

PAKISTAN

Madeline Donaldson

Lerner Publications Company • Minneapolis

Lerner Publications Company
A division of Lerner Publishing Group, Inc.
241 First Avenue North
Minneapolis, MN 55401 U.S.A.

Website address: www.lernerbooks.com

Library of Congress Cataloging-in-Publication Data

Donaldson, Madeline.
    Pakistan / by Madeline Donaldson.
      p.   cm. — (Country explorers)
    Includes index.
    ISBN 978–1–58013–599–3 (lib. bdg. : alk. paper)
    1. Pakistan—Juvenile literature. I. Title.
  DS376.9.D66 2009
  954.91—dc22   2008008726

Manufactured in the United States of America
1 2 3 4 5 6 – PA – 14 13 12 11 10 09

Table of Contents

Welcome!

You've just reached Pakistan! This country is on the continent of Asia. Southern Pakistan touches the Arabian Sea. To the west are the countries of Iran and Afghanistan. Northeast of Pakistan is China. Pakistan's eastern neighbor is India. India and Pakistan share a lot of history.

Pakistan

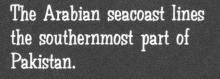

The Arabian seacoast lines the southernmost part of Pakistan.

4

mountains
valley
desert
plateau
country's capital
ancient cities

CHINA

HINDU KUSH

KARAKORAM RANGE

K2

HIMALAYAS

GILGIT RIVER

INDUS RIVER

NORTH-
WEST
FRONTIER
PROVINCE

KASHMIR

KABUL RIVER

Islamabad

AFGHANISTAN

JHELUM RIVER

Lahore

CHENAB RIVER

BALUCHISTAN
PLATEAU

Harappa

SUTLEJ RIVER

PUNJAB

PAKISTAN

INDUS RIVER VALLEY

INDUS RIVER

MILES
100
0   200

0   100   200   300
KILOMETERS

BALUCHISTAN

Mohenjo-Daro

INDIA

IRAN

THAR DESERT

SINDH

Karachi

ARABIAN
SEA

The Best River Ever

The Indus River flows down central Pakistan. It is one of the world's major rivers. Without water from the Indus, Pakistan would be mostly dry. With the water, the country can grow a lot of food.

Farms line the edge of the Indus River. The Indus River travels southward before emptying into the Arabian Sea.

The Indus is about 1,800 miles (2,897 kilometers) long. Shorter rivers feed into the Indus. They swell the Indus's waters. By the time it reaches the Arabian Sea, the Indus is huge!

Map Whiz Quiz

Take a look at the map on page 5. A map is a drawing or chart of a place. Trace the outline of Pakistan on a sheet of paper. See if you can find the Arabian Sea. Mark this part of your map with an *S* for *south*. How about India? Mark this side with an *E* for *east*. With a green crayon, color in Pakistan. Color China, Iran, and Afghanistan yellow to show where they end and Pakistan begins.

Two men cross the Indus River on a wooden footbridge.

Snow covers the peaks of these tall mountains.

Four Areas

Pakistan has four major land areas. They are the mountains in the north, the Indus River Valley, the Baluchistan Plateau, and the coast along the Arabian Sea.

The weather differs in the four areas. The north can get cold in winter. Snow stays on the tallest peaks all year. The valley gets most of the country's rain. But summers are hot. Farms do well in this area. The flat plateau is hot, dry, and hard to farm. Summer at the seacoast is hot too. At other times, though, wind from the sea cools the area.

Crops grow in one of Pakistan's many valleys.

K2

K2 lies within the Karakoram Range. It's the world's second-highest mountain. K2 rises 28,250 feet (8,610 meters) into the sky.

In the Mountains

Several mountain ranges cover northern Pakistan. The ranges include the Hindu Kush, the Karakoram, and the Himalayas.

Snow surrounds the K2 peak in the Karakoram Range.

The Karakoram Highway winds through the mountains of Pakistan. It runs for about 800 miles (1,300 km) from northern Pakistan to China and beyond.

The western province, or state, in this area is the North-West Frontier Province, or NWFP. Gaps between the mountains, called passes, let people and goods travel through the tall ranges.

In the Valley

The Indus River divides central Pakistan into two parts. The eastern part includes the provinces of Sindh and Punjab. They hold the Indus River Valley.

Women harvest wheat in Sindh province. Water from the Indus River helps Pakistan's rice and wheat crops thrive.

The Indus River Valley's farms raise huge crops of rice and wheat. In the south, the valley meets the Thar Desert. Most of this desert is in India.

A man rides a camel through the Thar Desert.

Western Pakistan

The western part of Pakistan is mainly a plateau. This region spreads over most of the province of Baluchistan.

This village is part of Baluchistan Province.

The Baluchistan Plateau has some low mountains and a few rivers. But mostly, it is dry and rugged. Not much farming happens there. But it's a great place for raising cattle, sheep, and goats.

By the Sea

The Indus River empties into the Arabian Sea. The coast along the Arabian Sea makes it easy to trade goods.

Ships sail past a new dock at a Pakistani seaport.

Ships bring in goods that Pakistan needs. Other ships take Pakistan's extra food and goods to other countries.

A boy guards a pile of eels ready to be taken to the fish market.

These children live in Punjab.

Pakistanis

The peoples that make up Pakistan match up with the provinces. Punjabis are the largest ethnic group. They mostly live in Punjab. Their language is called Panjabi. The Sindhi speak Sindhi and live in Sindh. Pathans are the main group in the NWFP. Their language is Pashto. And the Baluchi are in Baluchistan. Their language is also called Baluchi.

Sounds simple, right? Nope. These languages are different. Pakistan needed a language for everyone. The government chose Urdu as an official language. The country's many ethnic groups could easily learn it. They could use Urdu to speak to one another. Many Pakistanis also speak English, another official language.

This sign gives directions in both English and Urdu.

The ruins of the city of Mohenjo-Daro include houses and a tower.

Long-Ago Pakistan

About forty-five hundred years ago, ancient cities were near the Indus River. Scientists have uncovered two main cities. Harappa was in modern-day Punjab. Mohenjo-Daro was in modern-day Sindh.

The people who lived there were very clever. Both cities had plumbing in their neighborhoods. The streets were wide and sometimes paved. The people had a way of writing that still hasn't been figured out.

Visitors to Harappa can walk along ancient paved streets.

Becoming Pakistan

The British controlled Pakistan in the 1700s. The British ruled India and Pakistan together. Back then, these nations were not separate countries.

The people of India and Pakistan followed two main religions—Hinduism and Islam. Muslims (the followers of Islam) and Hindus worked to win freedom from British rule. They wanted to create two countries. Pakistan would be mainly Muslim. India would be mainly Hindu.

Muslims pray at a place of worship in the city of Lahore.

On August 14, 1947, Pakistan won its freedom from Britain. Pakistan and India finally split. Muslims throughout India moved to Pakistan.

Kashmir

When Pakistan and India split, they could not agree who would control Kashmir. Both sides wanted to control this area. India and Pakistan still don't agree on Kashmir. Fighting has broken out over the area.

Soldiers stand guard in the northeastern part of Kashmir.

Linked by Islam

Pakistan has many ethnic groups. They speak their own languages. They have different histories. But what links all the groups is the religion of Islam.

Boys study religious books at an Islamic place of worship in Lahore.

Almost all Pakistanis are Muslims. They pray five times daily to Allah (God). And they celebrate Islamic holidays throughout the year.

Old and New

Pakistan has two huge mosques (Islamic places of worship). The Badshahi Mosque in Punjab was finished in 1676. In 1976, builders started the Shah Faisal Mosque in the capital Islamabad. It has room for nearly a hundred thousand visitors!

Muslims pray in front of the Badshahi Mosque.

Celebrate!

Muslims throughout Pakistan honor the holy month of Ramadan. They fast from sunrise until sunset during this time. That means they do not eat or drink.

When the month ends, they hold a festival called Eid al-Fitr. Children get gifts. Women and girls decorate their hands with *mehndi*, a reddish dye. Workers receive extra money. Families get together for a special meal.

A girl prays outside a mosque in Karachi. Her hands are decorated with mehndi.

Men and boys gather to pray during Eid al-Azha. This festival honors the prophet Abraham. He was willing to give up his son to obey Allah. Other Islamic festivals honor the prophet Muhammad, who founded Islam.

A choir sings national songs during a celebration of Pakistan's independence day.

All in the Family

Most Pakistani families are large. Grandparents, parents, and married children may live in the same household. Younger family members honor those who are older.

A large family gathers in northern Pakistan.

28

Family ties are important. They can help children find marriage partners or get jobs. Family businesses may bring together the youngest to the oldest members. The whole family works hard to take care of one another.

This family runs a tailor shop. The grandfather, father, uncle, and son all work in the same place.

Islamabad

Pakistan took a while to set up Islamabad, its national capital city. In 1961, the government started building in the foothills of the Himalayas. Because builders started fresh, Islamabad is carefully planned and modern.

City Life

About one-third of Pakistanis live in cities. But the number is growing fast. People from the countryside move to cities to find jobs. Sometimes they open their own small businesses. These shops may sell goods such as pottery, linens, or jewelry.

Boys ride a taxi in Lahore. Most Pakistanis do not have cars, so they use taxis and buses.

The largest cities are Karachi and Lahore. Karachi's port is always very busy. The city's many factories make clothing, chemicals, and other goods. Lahore dates from hundreds of years ago. At that time, it was a major trade center. Lahore also has big universities and factories.

Dear Aunt Mary,

We just came back from the Shalimar Gardens in Lahore. The ruler who built India's Taj Mahal built them too. So they're really old! We saw all kinds of flowers and fruit trees. There were lots of ponds and waterfalls. Tomorrow we're going to Harappa. It's even older than the gardens. I can't wait!

See you soon!

Shalimar Gardens

Country Life

About two-thirds of Pakistanis live in the countryside. Many of them farm or raise animals.

Children play in a mountain valley in northern Pakistan. They have a net for fishing.

Kids have chores on the farms. Some families make goods, such as carpets or pottery, to sell at the local markets. Children help with this work too.

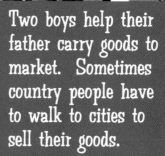

Two boys help their father carry goods to market. Sometimes country people have to walk to cities to sell their goods.

At the Bazaars

Bright reds, oranges, blues, and yellows catch the eye in Pakistan's bazaars. Most of the goods are handmade. Tall stacks of fruit and vegetables are homegrown.

34

Markets are often divided by what's being sold. People stroll in lanes where gleaming copper pots and pans are hanging. Silver and gold jewelry are grouped together. Another lane might have hand-knotted carpets. Next might come colorful pottery. Bolts of cloth might be in another area. Hand-sewn linens and clothing could be nearby.

This bazaar shop sells only bangles. Bangles are thin bracelets made of glass or metal.

Let's Eat!

Many foods in Pakistan are grown on the country's farms. Rice is served often. Pilau is lightly fried rice with vegetables and sometimes meat. A flat round bread, called chapati, is made of locally grown wheat.

These men sell chapatis in a bazaar. People sometimes use chapatis to scoop up and eat soft foods.

36

A salesman at a grocery store measures spices.

Meat—from the herds of sheep and cattle that thrive in Baluchistan and the NWFP—is also popular. Strong spices, such as garlic, curry, and ginger, give the meals snap!

Clothing

Most people in Pakistan wear long, loose cotton clothes. They keep people cool in the hot months.

Three girls wear loose cotton dresses on a hot day.

Some boys wear a shalwar-qamiz. Others wear T-shirts and pants. Still others have to wear school uniforms.

One common outfit is called the *shalwar-qamiz*. It's a knee-length shirt worn over baggy pants. Men and boys sometimes wear a vest over the shirt. Women often wrap a long scarf around their heads.

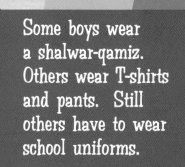

School

Pakistani children start school at about the age of five.
But only about half of the kids get to go to school.
More boys get the chance than girls.

Girls and boys listen to their teacher in a small classroom.

Often children don't stay in school past the early grades. Many kids stay home to help their families farm. Some have jobs in the family business.

RugMark

Some children in Pakistan weave rugs instead of going to school. The work is very hard. But the children get little money for their work. A group called RugMark is trying to help these children. This group rewards rug makers who don't hire kids. It allows the rug makers to attach a tag to their rugs. The tag says the rugs were not made by children.

These children help their parents with farmwork.

Sports

Kids in Pakistan often play cricket and field hockey. The British brought these games to Pakistan.

Hundreds of Pakistani children gather to play cricket on a field in Lahore.

Cricket is a bit like baseball. Field hockey is played on a grass field. Pakistani national teams have been successful in both sports.

The Pakistani national field hockey team lines up for practice in Islamabad.

THE FLAG OF PAKISTAN

Pakistan's flag is green and white. Muhammad Ali Jinnah designed it. He was the founder of Pakistan. The large green area stands for the country's Muslims. The smaller white stripe stands for non-Muslim Pakistanis. The half moon shape, called a crescent, stands for progress. The five-pointed star represents light and knowledge.

FAST FACTS

FULL COUNTRY NAME: Islamic Republic of Pakistan

AREA: 310,403 square miles (803,940 square kilometers), or about the size of Texas

MAIN LANDFORMS: the mountain ranges the Hindu Kush, the Karakoram, and the Himalayas; the Baluchistan Plateau; the Indus River Valley; the Thar Desert; the coast of the Arabian Sea

MAJOR RIVERS: Indus, Jhelum, Chenab, Sutlej, Gilgit, Kabul

ANIMALS AND THEIR HABITATS: crocodiles (rivers); snow leopards, Marco Polo sheep (northern mountains); jackals, hyenas, blackbuck (deserts)

CAPITAL CITY: Islamabad

OFFICIAL LANGUAGES: Urdu and English

POPULATION: about 169,300,000

GLOSSARY

ancient: very old

bazaar: street market

continent: any one of seven large areas of land. The continents are Africa, Antarctica, Asia, Australia, Europe, North America, and South America.

desert: a dry, sandy region

ethnic group: a large community of people that share the same language, religion, and customs

goods: things to sell

Islam: a religion that began in Saudi Arabia. Followers of Islam worship Allah.

map: a drawing or chart of all or part of Earth or the sky

mosque: an Islamic place of worship

mountain: a part of Earth's surface that rises high into the sky

Muslim: a follower of Islam

pass: a large gap between mountains that lets travelers pass through

plateau: a high, flat area of land

port: a place on the water where boats can dock

province: a region within a country. Provinces are like U.S. states.

valley: an area of low land that gets its water from a large river

TO LEARN MORE

BOOKS

Douglass, Susan L. *Ramadan.* Minneapolis: Millbrook Press, 2004. Learn about the month of Ramadan, during which Muslims around the world—including Pakistanis—honor Allah.

Mobin-Uddin, Asma. *The Best Eid Ever.* Honesdale, PA: Boyds Mills Press, 2007. This book tells the story of a girl's celebration of Eid al-Azha with her grandmother.

Razzak, Shazia. *P Is for Pakistan.* London: Frances Lincoln, 2007. Going through the alphabet, this book shows the people and culture of Pakistan in colorful photos.

Sharth, Sharon. *Pakistan.* Chanhassen, MN: Child's World, 2003. You can find out more about the culture of Pakistan with this title.

WEBSITES

Enchanted Learning
http://www.enchantedlearning.com/geography
This site has pages to label and color of Pakistan and its flag.

Harappa
http://www.harappa.com
This fantastic site has hundreds of images from both Harappa and Mohenjo-Daro. It also tells the story of Pakistan before it became a country in 1947.

INDEX

The images in this book are used with the permission of: © Aamir Qureshi/AFP/Getty Images, pp. 4, 16, 27, 43; © Bill Hauser/Independent Picture Service, all page illustrations, p. 5; © Tibor Bognar/Art Directors, pp. 6, 18; © Galen Rowell/CORBIS, p. 7; © Martin Barlow/Art Directors, p. 8; © Robert Harding/ Robert Harding World Imagery/Getty Images, p. 9; © Trip/Art Directors, pp. 10, 31, 38; © age fotostock/SuperStock, pp. 11, 21; © Nadeem Khawer/EPA/ CORBIS, p. 12; © Cory Langley, pp. 13, 15, 33, 36, 39; © Fabienne Fossez/Alamy, p. 14; © Neil McAllister/Alamy, pp. 17, 19; © Robin Graham/Art Directors, p. 20; © Juliet Highet/Art Directors, pp. 22, 29, 32; © Dario Mitidieri/Reportage/Getty Images, p. 23; © Hemis.fr/SuperStock, p. 24; AP Photo/K. M. Chaudary, p. 25; © Asif Hassan/AFP/Getty Images, pp. 26, 37; © Fiona Good/Art Directors, pp. 28, 34, 40; © Teressa Rerras, pp. 30, 41; © AFP/Getty Images, p. 35; © Paul Gilham/Getty Images, p. 42; © Laura Westlund/Independent Picture Service, p. 44.

Front Cover: © Scott Barbour/Getty Images